WRITING STORIES
ADVENTURE STORIES

Anita Ganeri

Heinemann
LIBRARY

Chicago, Illinois

Edited by Dan Nunn, Rebecca Rissman,
and Sian Smith
Designed by Joanna Hinton-Malivoire
Original illustrations © Capstone Global
Library 2013
Picture research by Ruth Blair
Production by Sophia Argyris
Originated by Capstone Global Library Ltd
Printed and bound in China by South China Printing
Company Ltd

ISBN: 978 1 4329 7529 6 (Hardback)
ISBN: 978 1 4329 7536 4 (Paperback)

17 16 15 14 13
10 9 8 7 6 5 4 3 2 1

Cataloging-in-Publication Data is available at the
Library of Congress website.
Ganeri, Anita, 1961-
  Adventure stories / Anita Ganeri.
    pages cm.—(Writing Stories)
  Includes bibliographical references and index.
  ISBN 978-1-4329-7529-6 (hb)—ISBN 978-1-4329-
7536-4 (pb) 1. Adventure stories—Authorship. 2.
Creative writing. I. Title.

PN3377.5.A37G36 2013
808.3'87—dc23   2012043077

Acknowledgments
We would like to thank the following for permission
to reproduce photographs: Alamy pp.5 (© Bernie
Pearson), 7 (© Maurice Savage); Shutterstock,
background images and design features, pp.4 (©
Monkey Business Images), 6 (© Thai Soriano), 8 (©
Kamira), 9 (© Volodymyr Goinyk), 11 (© nuttakit), 12
(© Platslee), 14 (© 1971yes), 16 (© meunierd), 20 (©
Kostyantyn Ivanyshen), 22 (© Cheryl Casey), 24 (©
Willyam Bradberry), 26 (© mppriv).

Cover photographs reproduced with permission of
Shutterstock: pirate ship (© PLRANG), paper and
rope (© Tischenko Irina), skull and crossbones (©
Russell Shively).

Every effort has been made to contact copyright
holders of material reproduced in this book. Any
omissions will be rectified in subsequent printings if
notice is given to the publisher.

All the Internet addresses (URLs) given in this book
were valid at the time of going to press. However,
due to the dynamic nature of the Internet, some
addresses may have changed, or sites may have
changed or ceased to exist since publication. While
the author and publisher regret any inconvenience
this may cause readers, no responsibility for any
such changes can be accepted by either the author
or the publisher.

Some words are shown in bold, **like this**. You can find out
what they mean by looking in the glossary.

Contents

Follow this symbol to read an adventure story.

What Is a Story?

A story is a piece of **fiction** writing. It tells the reader about made-up people, places, and events. Before you start writing a story, you need to pick a **setting**, some **characters**, and an exciting **plot**.

What kinds of stories do you like writing? There are many different types. You can write mystery stories, funny stories, fairy tales, scary stories, animal stories, and many others. This book is about writing adventure stories.

Writing an Adventure Story

When you write an adventure story, you can let your imagination run wild. Make sure that your story is packed with action and excitement. There can be lots of twists and turns in your **plot**.

An exciting story makes you want to keep reading.

An adventure story needs daring **characters**, such as pirates, superheroes, or knights. You can set the adventure anywhere, even in outer space. You can place it in the past, present, or future.

Ideas Notebook

Have you ever had a really good idea for a story, then forgotten it? Keep a notebook and pencil handy for scribbling down ideas. Then you will remember them when you are ready to write your story.

Explorers need to sail through icy waters on their way to the South Pole.

You can get ideas from books, the Internet, or your imagination. Something you see on TV may spark a great story idea. For example, the real-life adventure of an explorer setting off to the South Pole might make a good idea for a story.

Story Starter

A good story needs a strong beginning that grabs your readers' attention. It should make them want to continue reading. It is also where you introduce your main **characters**.

Can you turn any of these ideas into story starters?

- A girl dreams of being a pirate.
- An explorer sets off for the jungle.
- A boy finds a hidden door in his house.
- An astronaut lands on another planet.

AN ADVENTURE STORY

More than anything else, Polly wanted to be a pirate. She dressed up in pirate clothes. She had a toy parrot that sat on her shoulder.

"Good night, Polly," said Mom, as she tucked Polly into bed.

But Polly was already asleep. She was dreaming that she was Pirate Polly, sailing the seven seas on a mighty pirate ship ...

Introduce your main character, but don't give too much away.

Scene Setting

You need to decide where and when your story happens. This is called the **setting**. Think about what your setting looks, sounds, and even smells like. This will help bring your story to life for your readers. The setting for the story in this book is a pirate ship, like the one below.

Can you think of some words to describe the ship?

The pirate ship creaked loudly as it tipped and rolled on the waves. Flying from the mast was a Jolly Roger flag. It sent shivers down Polly's spine. She could smell old, unwashed clothes and taste salt spray on her lips. Polly clung on to the ship's rail and tried her best not to feel seasick.

 This pirate story is set in a time hundreds of years ago.

Character Building

The **characters** in your story need to be interesting. Your reader should believe in them and care about them. Figure out what your characters look like and how they think, feel, and behave. Make fact files, like the ones below, for your main characters.

Character fact file
Character: Polly
Age: 8
Looks like: Long, dark hair
Personality: A dreamer
Likes: Pirates; dressing up
Dislikes: Anything pink

Character fact file
Character: Pirate captain
Age: Old
Looks like: Pirate hat and eye patch; bushy beard
Personality: Loud; frightening
Likes: Treasure; fighting
Dislikes: Sharks; walking the plank

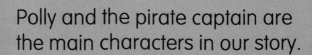

Polly and the pirate captain are the main characters in our story.

Suddenly, a large, loud figure appeared on deck. It was the pirate captain. He had a black, bushy beard and an eye patch. He held a shiny sword in his hand.

"Shiver me timbers!" he bellowed. "Pirate Polly, welcome on board!"

He gave Polly some pirate clothes to change into. Polly was too surprised to be scared.

In the Middle

The middle of your story is where the main action happens. It can be tricky to decide what happens next, especially if you have several ideas. Try using a **story map**, like the one below, to sort out your ideas.

What happens next?

1. Pirates sail to an island. They dig up a treasure chest.

2. Pirates sail to a treasure island. Their ship is wrecked on the rocks.

You need to decide which direction your story will go in.

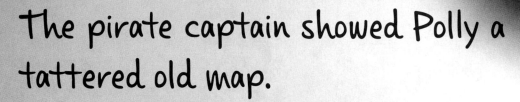

The pirate captain showed Polly a tattered old map.

"That's where we're heading—Treasure Island," he growled.

When they reached the island, the pirates started digging. They dug and dug all day. Finally, they dug up a big, wooden chest filled with jewels and gleaming gold coins.

"Hooray! We're rich!" shouted the captain, dancing a jig.

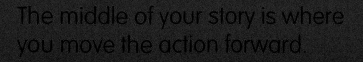
The middle of your story is where you move the action forward.

Tricky Problems

The middle of your story is also where something usually goes wrong for your **characters**. They have to find a way to solve their problems before the story ends. Here are some things that could go wrong for the pirates.

- The treasure chest falls overboard.
- The ship gets hit by a terrible storm.
- The ship is attacked by other pirates.
- The captain falls overboard into a sea full of sharks.

Can you think of any other problems?

The pirate ship set sail again.
But soon a terrible storm started.
The wind howled and the rain
lashed down. Polly was soaking
wet. Suddenly, a huge wave
crashed down on the deck ...
and washed the treasure chest
overboard into the swirling sea.

Speaking Parts

Dialogue means the words that people say. You can use it in your story to bring your **characters** to life. It can help to show what they are feeling and thinking. It is also useful for breaking up chunks of text.

"Treasure chest overboard!" yelled Polly. "What are we going to do now?"

Put **quotation marks** around the spoken words.

"Treasure chest overboard!" yelled Polly. "What are we going to do now?"

"There be nothing else for it," boomed the captain. "Ye'll have to go in after it."

"Me?" said Polly, in surprise. "But I've only just started going to swimming lessons. I can't even swim a whole length of the pool."

Bring the captain to life by making him speak more like a pirate.

Action Writing

Try to make your adventure story exciting and action-packed. You can do this by choosing your words carefully. For example, use interesting **verbs** ("doing words") as well as **adverbs** that describe how those things are done.

Polly quickly plunged into the sea.

Quickly is an adverb.
Plunged is a verb.

"Ye'll be fine," shouted the captain, loudly. "As long as ye mind out for sharks."

Gloomily, Polly stared into the water. It was dark, choppy, and full of pointy fins. She shivered.

"Come on," yelled the captain. "We don't have all day."

Polly took a deep breath, closed her eyes, and quickly plunged into the sea.

Happy Ending

What happens at the end of your story? This is where you tie up any loose ends and your **characters** solve their problems. They may live happily ever after, but the ending can also be sad or have a surprising twist for the reader.

Endings

- Polly is made queen of the sharks.
- Polly beats the sharks and finds the chest.
- Polly is eaten by sharks.
- Polly wakes up and finds that it has all been a dream.

Here are some possible endings to the story in this book.

"I almost have it," called Polly, as her fingers closed on the chest.

She looked up and stared straight into the eyes of a shark ...

"Polly! Polly!" came Mom's voice. "You're having a funny dream."

Polly opened her eyes and blinked. It was morning. The pirates had gone and she was in her room. Best of all, there was not a shark to be seen. What an adventure it had been!

Try writing a different ending to this story.

More Top Tips

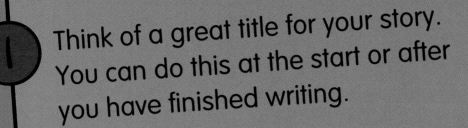

1 Think of a great title for your story. You can do this at the start or after you have finished writing.

2 Read your story out loud to make sure that it flows and sounds right. An adventure story should be exciting through to the end.

3 Tell your story from a different point of view. For example, you could retell this story in Polly's voice.

4 Your story will probably not come out right the first time. Be ready to rewrite it several times until it is perfect.

5 If you get stuck, try some automatic writing. Write down anything that comes into your head and see what happens.

6 Read lots of other adventure stories. This will help you with your **plot** and **characters** and make your writing better.

Glossary

adverb describing word that tells you about a verb

character person in a piece of writing

dialogue words that characters say

fiction piece of writing that is about made-up places, events, and characters

plot what happens in a story

quotation marks marks that show the words someone has spoken

setting time and place in which a story is set

story map diagram that helps you decide the next step of the plot

story mountain mountain-shaped diagram that helps you plan out a story

timeline list of events in the order in which they happen

verb doing or action word

Find Out More

Books

Ganeri, Anita. *Writing Stories*. Chicago: Raintree, 2013.

Stowell, Louie, and Jane Chisholm. *Write Your Own Story Book*. Tulsa, Okla.: EDC, 2011.

Warren, Celia. *How to Write Stories* (How to Write). Laguna Hills, Calif.: QEB, 2007.

Web sites

Facthound offers a safe, fun way to find Internet sites related to this book. All of the sites on Facthound have been researched by our staff.

Here's all you do:
Visit **www.facthound.com**
Type in this code: 9781432975296.

Index